Christian History Detective

Essays, Analysis and Musings on Primary

Source Documents and Related

Historical Matters

By Rev. James DuJack

ISBN:0615815502

ISBN-13:9780615815503

ACKNOWLEDGEMENT AND DEDICATION:

The foregoing is a series of unedited essays assigned for a course called "History of Christianity" at the Alliance Theological Seminary. The opinions expressed are mine alone and do not reflect the views of the seminary, denomination or the Professors. I would like to acknowledge and dedicate this work to Professor Julie Cox, Professor Christopher Dost and Professor Lyndell O'Hara, each of whom has made my return to seminary after a thirty year hiatus a challenge and a joy. Finally, I give thanks to Advisor and Professor William Crockett who not only predated me at ATS but looks and plays the part of detective very well.

CONTENTS

ESSAY 1: THE DIDACHE

The Didache is a source of instruction that I have been familiar with for many years. For me its flavor is reminiscent of James, which I believe to be written as among the earliest of the New Testament writings. As such, the Didache reads like a combination of a catechism and an operations manual. It has a distinctly and decidedly "didactic" feel. Like James, it does not contain much by way of any precise or well developed Christology, and little of what we might call "formal theology". It does, however, possess a great deal of "practical theology" as in a focus on "social ethics". Its opening "two ways" is reminiscent of Psalm One, which betray (for many) an origin familiar with Jewish roots. What has stood out in this most recent re-read of the Didache is the really remarkable lack of much referencing of the name of Jesus. Especially in light of the great importance the New Testament places on His "name". While the Son is depicted with titles of many sorts, and the language unmistakably points to Him, there are but a few (4?) "verbatim" mentions of "Jesus" (at least it seems so in this translation). Further, each of these mentions are found only by way of prayers to be recited. "Jesus" is not mentioned until Chapter 9, (three times) and Chapter 10 (once). I found this most intriguing.

My re-read also reminded me of a couple of things I have found to be rather odd concerning the Didache. Some of these I will elaborate on in the sections following. One oddity however, really stands out. I find it most curious that the Didache veritably opens with (not a power punch but) a limp, deflated, and truncated version of the Golden Rule. Jesus said "Do unto others… " , the Didache says "Do not do…"! Jesus knew that dead people could "not do unto others" and cited the Pharisees as those not teaching or living up to the positive command to "do". Between these two versions (positive and negative), there is a world of difference. Anyhow, onto our four sections.

I.   Throughout the entirely of the Didache, there is a sense that fellow believers are, and are to be a precious, close-knit group. The "my child" that opens Chapter three and four expresses the attitude that permeates the instruction. Indeed, the Didache is instruction and instructive. First, we can sense and learn that our ATTITUDE is not disconnected from our ACTIONS. Hence the strong overtones concerning hypocrisy. While the Didache concerns itself largely with Godly actions, these are simply the "how-to's", as in, "how to" love one another. Second, as we (contemporaries) sadly "celebrate" the 40th anniversary of Roe vs. Wade, we see the way of life celebrated in the Didache, with an explicit command prohibiting abortion. At the same time, the Didache provides protective warnings against false brethren. There is considerable wariness displayed over the motivations and intention of others. The brethren are alerted to be on guard concerning themselves and others. Again, as actions speak louder than words, practical parameters are placed to give guidance. Some of these seem to be rather arbitrary, yet no doubt there were contextual circumstances which gave rise. All of these same factors and conditions are true of how the Didache instructs concerning leaders: bishops, deacons, prophets. Since the author(s) of the Didache knows that leadership is critical (and how much of a blessing or curse it can be), greater guidance is on display. Whole chapters are committed to this topic; Chapters 6, 11, 13, and 15. I offer as an aside the fact that the author(s) of the Didache might not be very happy with me. Two weekends ago I hosted a visiting minister for THREE days. Yet, I do not esteem him a false prophet! Closing out this segment, the Didache rightly (very consistent with the New Testament) enjoins that great honor and esteem be given for those found worthy in their ministerial calling and duties.

II.   The Sacramental rites of Baptism and the Eucharist were, and are very important, as the Didache reveals. The degree to which there was (to the modern mind) a high level of importance placed on the particulars of the prescribed prayers reveals just how important these rites were! I was particularly moved by the emphasis on "gathered together" during the communion rite, even as the bread was broken and "scattered". I also wish that more Ministers and Christians today would heed the instruction concerning Baptism as a rite of initiation with communion ONLY for those so initiated. There seems to be a wide-scale breakdown in modern times of the significance of Baptism as covenant initiation and Communion as covenant renewal.

III.   As the wariness addressed in section one reveals, there seems to have been a major problem with scam and sham artists in the early Church. Second only to honoring God and guarding oneself, the early Christians were heavily warned in the Didache to be on the watch-out for unscrupulous characters. Again we see (whether seemingly or genuinely arbitrary) VERY specific and detailed specifications listed as guidelines. Honest living vs. hypocrisy seems to be a dominant theme. Honest living also includes honest and hard WORK! Of course, the brethren are also to be on the lookout for false TEACHING as well as those false teachers. The instruction on reproof, reception, and methods of reconciliation show that the early Church was not exempt from the common "people problems" that plague the Church to this day.

IV.   The spiritual disciplines practiced included assembly, support, prayer, and fasting. These last two, the subject of Chapter eight, are again highly regulated and mechanically and meticulously specific, which seem odd. Of course, (with respect to fasting), one can be a hypocrite on any day of the week! Perhaps the real instruction is about being aware of associations? Not only is fasting addressed in a problematic way, but we ought not be like the hypocrites concerning vain repetitions. One could easily make the case that the Didache SEEMS to allow for, if not promote vain repetition. For sure these practices tangent the practices and disciplines of our day. A larger discussion would be needed to search out if and/or how these particular prescriptions have contextual circumstances which gave them birth thereby potentially making them "legitimately" helpful and valid instructions OR if these at root are at odds with the teaching and spirit of the New Testament. As for me, I'd like to cut the author(s) some slack, and I tend to think, even hope, that God has done just that.

ESSAY 2: THE LETTERS OF IGNATIUS

The letters of Ignatius mark him not only as a product OF his times, but as one sent from God FOR his times. Fond of his surname: Theophorus, Ignatius both carried God's name, and was carried by God. The reading of his letters reveal him to be both a towering figure in terms of charting the course for early church history, and a tender devotee of Jesus, who set him free.

On his way to martyrdom in Rome, important and revealing letters were written. The excerpts from the letters to the Ephesians and the Magnesians provide great insight into the establishment of "office based" church order in the early church. The letter to the Romans is a touching portrayal of one joyfully at peace "to be an imitator of the passion" of God through martyrdom.

Concerning the former, Ignatius powerfully posits the establishment of the church hierarchy as good and Godly. He also posits this beautifully. Not only is this well done, but done with artistic even aesthetically beautiful metaphors throughout. Following his "Prince of Peace", the Lord Jesus Christ, Ignatius implores peaceful harmony. His vision of church order is "harmony" and is filled with musical terminology. There is a steady stream of "refrain" (pun intended) of the "harmonious" … with "strings to a harp", and "choir", composed of "blending in concert", as "sung", in "key-note to God". These are, most definitely, not the typical terms utilized when a structure of authority the likes of which he set forth is presented! Yet this is how Ignatius posits the good and Godly government of church rule by Her bishops. It would be easy to simply discount him merely as a product OF his times; though he was that for sure! Yet, at least as important, would be to view him as an agent (gift) from God FOR his times. With no established canon, (and microscopic literacy rates even had there been established written authority and written material available) with Gnostic enemies (at the least in their incipient stage) abounding, there was so great a need, and so great a vacuum of established authority! Into this age, and into this void, and in this regard, Ignatius served as a "necessary man". As such, he served with distinction, when the Church most certainly faced possible, even probable (humanly speaking) extinction! It is the likes of Ignatius to whom the Church owes a debt of gratitude as for Her very survival. The question of course emerges; what does this mean NOW (for bishops and hierarchy) that written authority does exist, and is available, and is read by the masses?

Let us not get too far ahead. Back to Ignatius. He set the bishops as the THEN "bridge" between God and mankind. Whereas, democracy has cried, "the voice of the people is the voice of God"; Ignatius veritably cried, "the voice of the bishop is the voice of God". In the time of transition from Jesus Christ as the Word, … to the TEXT of Scripture, Ignatius set forth … the bishops. This honor and this role, the bishops indeed were to have and to play, and, owing to their office, were to perform and to be reckoned, as unto Christ Himself. As such, neither their youth nor any other human factor should lessen ones regard for them. They were to be honored, heard, loved, and obeyed. Even as Christ Himself. Harmony with THEM was viewed as harmony with Christ and God.

Having once heard an old saying; "there can be no harmony, unless someone is willing to play second fiddle" (attributed to Leonard Bernstein, the late conductor of New York Philharmonic Symphony), I can imagine Ignatius singing that tune and imploring Christians to do just that. The Church harmony he sought was dependent upon the roles (and tune) played by both bishop and laity (first and second fiddle) alike!

Equally powerful and beautiful were the martyrdom meditations of Ignatius's letter to the Romans. This letter, as well as those addressed prior, reveal a touch of literary artistry. Ignatius uses "wild beasts" in literal and figurative fashion, (like St. Paul in 1 Corinthians 15:32) to paint a picture both of his human (inhumane) enemies (escorts), and the likely literal lion's den he would soon find himself in, as the means of his execution. More powerful and more beautiful than his poetry (his death as a sunset, his resurrection as a sunrise) and prose, was his preparation and peace concerning his fate.

Common (perhaps too common?) to his time was not only the "willingness" toward martyrdom for Christ, but also a seeming "wantingness". In our discussion board of a week ago, comment was made concerning what I'll call "this strange motivation". Emphasis in that discussion board was made that ours ought to be an orientation of LIFE because Jesus DIED for us, not a (sprint) race toward death to reveal some sort of special identification with Him! It does seem that alive and perhaps too well was a "strange motivation" toward martyrdom!

To this matter, I say; each to his/her own calling. Nevertheless, Ignatius, as true to the times (in certain circles) seemed to possess this overt wantingness in addition to his willingness. Of course, it also should be noted that, "wantingness" makes perfect sense and may be a preferable path if/as this was a foregone conclusion! A question in my mind is as follows: In a passage, (such as chapter 7) which may sound to be "Gnostic" in orientation; is that sentiment owing to:

  a) His desire to be (where Christ is) with Christ?
  b) That same foregone conclusion of martyrdom?
  c) The desire to be released from pain?
  d) All of the above?
  e) None of the above?
  f) Some of the above?

Contained in this letter, and tied into his martyrdom is a curious and repeated use of the word and concept of "ATTAINING unto God" and/or "ATTAINING unto Jesus Christ". This certainly seems to have soteriological significance. Are issues of assurance at play? Are there issues of "works" at play? Is the very issue of martyrdom as a guarantee of salvation an issue at play?

Ignatius certainly viewed martyrdom for Christ as among the highest of honors to be bestowed upon a Christian. Ignatius certainly viewed his soon to be martyrdom as a badge of honor, and one for all Christians to be prepared for and at peace with. In terms of faith, discipleship, and martyrdom, I think Ignatius viewed them all as one. He did live (and die), and he would have all Saints live; as overcomers; …"by the blood of the Lamb, and by the word of their testimony; and they loved not their lives unto the death". Revelation 12:11.

What Bonhoeffer (who literally wrote the book on "The Cost Of Discipleship") advocated, seems like a walk in the park compared to the example and teaching set forth by Ignatius, Bishop of Antioch!

ESSAY 3: THE NESTORIAN TABLET

Has there been written a more beautiful depiction of the glory and the blessing of the Christian Faith (there and then) known as the Illustrious Religion; than the Nestorian Tablet?

All one can say is "WOW".

Self- described as "a eulogy of their magnanimous deeds", the Nestorian Tablet recounts the considerable impact of the Christian Faith and her followers throughout the empire of China, as the "Illustrious breezes (that) have come to fan the East". Erected in A.D. 781, this stone tablet commemorates the history and triumphs of the Christian Faith in that region during the seventh and eighth centuries.

As a westerner, Calvin's Geneva was thought to be the pinnacle of the idyllic achievements Christendom could bring to a society. Yet in the Tablet, there is revealed a society and culture which reduces the fondest considerations of Geneva to a mere "also ran" or an "after thought"; perhaps deserving of an "honorable mention". Perhaps.

Turning to an analysis of the beliefs and values of Nestorianism; while marked in history (by many) as OUTSIDE the Christian Faith, there is much to make of viewing it as a branch OF the Christian Faith. Labeled as heretical by the Council of Ephesus, Nestorianism represents a (failed) attempt to give (satisfactorily orthodox) expression to the "nature(s)" of Jesus the Christ. Connected to any discussion of the "nature(s)" of Jesus would be the related issues of (multiple?) "personhood". As no single component of Christology remains in isolation, Nestorianism also necessarily impacted how the Virgin Mary ought to be addressed. The Nestorians favored "Christokos"; Christ-bearer over "Theotokos"; God-bearer. Here again, Ephesus ruled against the Nestorian position. These Christological matters concerning the "mystical/hypostatic union" of the divine and human natures, and how they impacted personhood were further taken up at Chalcedon. Perhaps Nestorius's greatest error was in trying to articulate that which is near impossible to articulate. It is an understatement of considerable proportion to say that the incarnation presents incredibly formidable challenges to metaphysical and ontological understandings and expressions. More than a thousand years AFTER Chalcedon, Charles Wesley was still penning lyrics which reveal this challenge; "Tis mystery all, the Immortal dies, who can explore His strange design?.....Let angel minds inquire no more." Another hymn writer (M. Bridges) of the same period cited the wonders of the essence and nature of God as "Ineffably sublime".

As for me, therefore, I prefer to cut them some slack and view the Nestorians more as a branch of the faith. I am not hereby affirming their position or minimizing the theological consequences of their position. Nor is a proper understanding (and expression) of Christology a matter to be trifled with. Perhaps I am becoming a softie in my riper years, but if we are to know them by their fruits, then the Nestorians (whatever else we may make of their erroneous views) are my brothers and sisters.

But alas, the Nestorians were clear; Christ was divided, even as we read in the "Ode". The Church, therefore, wanting (insisting) the Christological emphasis to remain one of "union", could not abide the Nestorian position. What is fascinating for me is that in the arena of understanding and expressing the Trinity (which is perhaps an even greater mystery and mental conundrum), the Nestorians remain orthodox. It is for a mind far greater than mine to draw conclusions concerning whether or not their doctrinal deficiencies played a role in their veritable demise. Were those deficiencies deadly to the movement? God alone is Lord of history.

Setting aside the above addressed issue of Christology, the Nestorians appear largely and uniformly orthodox. Some Church related issues of concern might include the following. From the Tablet, if pressed, I might pursue their concepts of "primordial substance" and creation, and their practice of worship and praise for "the dead"? Also of note, though the Tablet does not claim to be an exhaustive treatment of ALL that the Nestorians practiced, it did seem to be a peculiar omission that there was no clear mention of a Communion Rite. Was the Table absent from their practice OR simply absent from the Tablet? On the positive side, the depiction of the beard as symbolizing outward action and the shaved crown as the absence of inward affection marked them as an army in the world, but not of the world. Some of the best and most Biblical practices one could find anywhere on earth and in history were on display. The initiation rite of Baptism, the attitudes concerning wealth, poverty, and charity, as well as equality all seemed to be guided by, and within Biblical boundaries. Practices such as prayer, fasting, and Sabbath rest appeared to be widely embraced. Perhaps an undue superstitious "aid to worship" seems to have included the use of the cross. Whether figurative or otherwise, this use also resulted in positive works of benevolence to many. Such a people cannot help but be, and bring much blessing. The Eulogy and the Ode reveal the enormous benefits that flowed; from peace to prosperity. Likewise, joy, order, honor, stability all seemed to flourish during this time. Even the Hobbits of Tolkien's mythical "Shire" might enviously seek relocation if presented the opportunity.

How was this faith received? Save brief periods of opposition from Buddhists in A.D. 699 in the East, and from "base" elements in the west in A.D. 713, the Nestorians seemed very well received. With joy (generally), leader after leader energetically welcomed and advanced this movement. Becoming known as the Illustrious Religion, Nestorianism was revered as "excellent", "beneficial", advantageous" and "laudable". Furthermore, its influences and representatives were "able to counteract noxious influences". (This sort of makes one wonder if it were also effective in combating influenza; just kidding). Returning to all seriousness; what a testimony, this broad and tall (10 feet) Tablet! A testimony to Jesus! A testimony to the truth! A testimony to the Church as the people of God! Few documents have moved me to the degree this one has. Representing what has occurred in history, this Tablet is a sure encouragement, and motivation as to what can be in the future, even in this fallen and sinful world.

Though I fully support the necessary and difficult work of my fore fathers in the Church, and in the findings of our historic Councils, and I respect the desire and duty to uphold all doctrinal purity and precision, I also am proud to reckon the Nestorians as among the dearest of brothers and sisters in Christ.

ESSAY 4: THE NICENE CREED & COUNCIL

Shortly following the Edict of Milan (A.D. 313) wherein there was promised the reduction of threats to the Church from without, disagreements within the Church threatened the peace and unity so many had hoped for, including the Emperor Constantine. Like so many of the internal conflicts that had already plagued the Church, a new major one, (about A.D. 320) had its origin in "subordinationist" views concerning Jesus the Christ. Arius, an elder at Alexandria, began to propagate and popularize (he was a marketing genius) his idea that Jesus was not quite of the same essence as God the Father. This form of subordinationist thinking concerned principally Jesus' creation; begotten before time, yet "there was when the Son was not." This marked Jesus as SOMETHING other, and less than God. This was most unsettling, as it was an obvious threat to the understanding of the divinity of the Son, an understanding at the core of the Christian Faith. Exacerbating this problem was the heretofore mentioned acknowledgement that Arius was a marketing genius. Sung in the bars and along the byways of Alexandria were various musical "ditties" composed around his doctrines. So formidable (and popular) were these songs and doctrines, that Council was called, (A.D. 325) gathering Bishops, (some 300 in number) from around the world, both East and West, to Nicaea. Though most certainly an important (and explosive) part of Church history, the full exploration of which is a tad outside the scope of this essay, the role of Constantine, the Emperor in calling, convening, and providing coordination and "counsel" during this Council, is itself a most fascinating subject!

Emerging from this Council was the Nicene Creed. This was a historic landmark achievement! As our textbook and so many other sources cite, the "same substance" (homoousios) language was introduced (but not invented), argued, and prevailed. This was not without controversy and intrigue of its own with the role of Constantine, the influence of Bishop Hosius, and the irksome connotations of Paul of Samosta, all at play. Also emerging from this Council was the repudiation of Arius. That, however, was not nearly the end of the story. Though the anti-Arian position was overwhelmingly adopted and the Creed composed, several Bishops and Constantine himself found themselves in various forms of pro-Arius support positions over the ensuing years. The settled peace and unity Constantine hoped for was not to be soon found. A more moderate form of Arianism (called Semi-Arianism) took hold. They advanced the use of "similar substance" (homoiousios) to best communicate the essence of Jesus in relation to the Father. It is during this post-Nicaea time frame that the metal was tested of Athanasius, (who had served in an advisory capacity at Council) as Bishop of Alexandria for the subsequent half century. Battling Arius (who died in A.D. 335, another whole story unto itself) and this newfangled Semi-Arianism was his life's work. "Athanasius Against The World" epitomized the immensity of his struggle for orthodoxy. To the mind of this writer, it not only epitomized his sense of sociological isolation, but also his theological commitment. Orthodoxy required him (and us) to hold to that which remains a mystery, and oppose the more (worldly) understandable and socially palatable forms of subordinationist theories. Hence, "Athanasius Against The World". It should be noted that though the language of the debate looked so much alike (homoousios/homoiousios), the difference and consequences are enormous, even infinite. With all due respect to our text author who wrote of "splitting important hairs", (I think he would agree, as at least he called them "important") this is not simply "splitting hairs". These are much more likened to hairs of a whole different animal! If the Son is different than the Father; then HOW MUCH different; and in WHAT WAYS different?

Nevertheless, (even as in the case of the Nestorians) it is easy to sympathize with the Arian desire to define and articulate Sonship. How else might one account for, and communicate a being (begotten?) "posterior" to God, if that be what Sonship requires? All human sympathies aside, our greatest allegiance must be to God, whose Son must be divine if He indeed brought salvation. This indeed was the basic issue comparing and contrasting the Sonship theologies of Arius and Athanasius. Unless it was missed in my assigned readings, an additional issue of intrigue was the emergence of a major Orthodox hymn (attributed to this time period) which came to be known as the Gloria Patri. This is intriguing because "song" was so instrumental (pardon the pun) to the advance of Arianism. Now groups could "taunt" each other with their competing "sung theologies." The lyric…"As it was in the beginning, is now and ever shall be" directly answers not only Trinitarian matters, but subsequent Christological ones, including the subordinationist plank citing that "there was when the Son was not."

Even though Arianism found support and voice for 50 years following Nicaea, the baseline foundational work done there, and reinforced through Athanasius was a key support making this decision such a bedrock of the Christian faith. The Nicene Creed and Council firmly established a ruling tradition concerning Christology against which all future subordinationists would have to fight and overcome. Without such a ruling and creedal statement, the entire Trinitarian formulation would be at risk and the Christian faith could potentially bear little resemblance to what it is today. The effect on theology, had the council decided in Arius's favor, would have been profound and far-reaching. First, as our text indicates (pg.104) it would mean a God (Father) who is removed from man, even unapproachable. I could envision a scenario unfolding where (the understanding of) our God devolved or degenerated into a Muslim-like god (who is aloof, removed, detached) and Jesus reduced in like measure to one such as Mohammed, a mere, albeit special messenger.

Second, devastating and irreparable damage would be done to the Trinitarian construct. This is no small concern. First, it would remove "the one and the many" philosophical orientation, (modeled in and by the Trinity) that has led to the remarkable progress and the governmental structures of Western culture. Next, it would very negatively impact the profound and positive "relational" aspects of our faith, which again is modeled in and by the Trinity. Going out on a limb here, I surmise that without Nicaea… or something equivalent thereafter, that the doctrine concerning the Person and the work of the Holy Spirit would have been difficult to maintain.

In closing summary: by virtue of the Church bravely submitting to revealed mystery, instead of submitting only to that which can be measured by the mind of mankind; the Church has provided us with a glorious heritage (instead of a man-made religion) and one sure to endure (as the Gloria Patri closes) "World Without End, Amen."

ESSAY 5: THE CONFESSIONS OF ST. AUGUSTINE

On display in brilliant array in the Confessions of St. Augustine is the truth of Scripture (Old and New Testament) proclaiming : "… we … believe, therefore (we) speak." (Psalm 116:10 and 2 Corinthians 4:13). The Confessions indeed represent the vocalization of that which faith generates. The Confessions are filled with prayer, praise, even questions as much as answers. The Confessions are also filled with Scripture (an emphasis I will later close with). Throughout the Confessions, the soul of St. Augustine is laid bare, but is not silent! To read the Confessions is as if Augustine had become the embodiment (on steroids) of what St. Anselm later (11th century) put to print; "faith seeking understanding". It therefore should not go unnoticed, that the Confessions also are, and contain a CRY … a pleading! From Psalm 35:3; (… "SAY unto my soul, I am thy salvation"), referenced repeatedly by Augustine, (at least twice; 1:5 and 9:1), the Confessions were as much about Augustine longing to HEAR from God, as they were about God (with us now listening in) HEARING from Augustine.

Reading through the Confessions, and especially the conversion account of Chapter (book) 8, Augustine is depicted as one who has lived through (in fullness) his own depiction of mankind; as those who are (paraphrasing here from Chapter 1:1) made for God, and therefore are restless until they find rest in Him. The restlessness of his post-conversion life was of a completely different sort than his pre-conversion restlessness. Whereas prior to conversion his restlessness was that of a lost, wandering, fearful, soul-less, yet beastly zombie, his post-conversion restlessness was an all-consuming exploration of his new found home and Father, the delights and wonders thereof knew no bounds. It is hard to imagine one reading the Confessions without coming to the conclusion of viewing Augustine as a man of the deepest devotion and affection for his Lord. If it be true that the tenderest of disciples make for the best teachers of doctrines, then Augustine certainly fills that bill.

Irony of ironies; that which St. Augustine believed concerning himself (in the flesh) as that which kept him from full commitment to God, actually was that which caused him to cling and cleave all the more unto God. His clinging and cleaving to God was tenacious, desperate, and perpetual. Augustine knew of his own fallen nature. This knowledge was not that (only) of a textbook or theoretical variety, (though he knew and held to THAT variety as well). Augustine continued to dwell with the intimate and personal awareness of his own awfulness and unworthiness. He continued to marvel (in horror), at his own sensual (particularly sexual) lustings. Like many (if not most) believers of his times, Augustine viewed perpetual celibacy as a superior spiritual path. Even more, he believed this to be the ONLY path for himself. Combining this "demand" with his own nature (as a man of like passions as we all are); Augustine was always held back in check in terms of sensing he had arrived or attained. This is the same spirit captivating St. Paul (Philippians 3:12), pushing both men forward. While I certainly think that Augustine was the victim of, and held defective views on sexuality, I also have no doubt but that his sexual energies were sublimated into profound accomplishments for the Church and Kingdom. Note: God uses even our perversions (faulty thinking) for His glory. This is a mysterious life-lesson, not a license.

It is no small thing for one such as I, to find fault with one such as St. Augustine on ANYTHING. Yet, with Augustine having been a man (not God), it is appropriate to consider at least the possibility of the specter of his errors and defective views. I am not sure that our PSE is the right place to pursue such, but better understanding of a full-orbed exegetical study of the New Testament use of the "flesh" with its considerable semantic range and nuances, might have led Augustine (and most others of his era) to some different conclusions.

The later (even centuries later), poetic depiction of "better angels" vs. "bad angels" might well communicate the good vs. evil battle of nature's waging war in the human (even Christian) heart, according to Augustine. All his days, he was convinced concerning the inherent sinfulness of man. Even his (prolonged:

nine year) stint with the Manicheans was no doubt wrapped up in his wrestling over the nature and origin of evil. Contrary to man, Augustine saw God as all good, and the ONLY good. This latter point forms the foundation for Augustinian soteriology. Like Luther after him (who, writing to Erasmus, said that the REAL issue of the Reformation was the "will of man"), and later Calvin (who advanced the "doctrines of grace"), Augustine was decidedly predestinarian. In this sense, Augustine's experience and teaching would contrast with the dominant presentation of the Gospel call today with its pronounced emphasis on what we might call "decisionism". Most unfortunately, the teachings of Pelagius (even more, Semi-Pelagianism) are very much alive and well today. Yet, in remarkable commonality to that which is widely advanced today was the "crisis/instantaneous/in a moment" translation of Augustine from the kingdom of darkness into the kingdom of light. These recognizable and remembered experiences are a MUST in many locations. Happily, since God's grace is greater, and His regenerative powers more diverse in application, heaven is not such a location where that type experience is among those that are a MUST. Heaven knows only that "you must be born again."

Though these primary source essays are not commonly the place for personal anecdotes and expressions, I will take the liberty (and exception) here to gladly recount some of my own "confession", even at the risk of losing assignment points. I write this because I was particularly moved by three things in Confessions:

1. How much the life of Augustine was saturated by Scripture.
2. The role at his point of conversion of the Scripture.
3. How with regard to the Scripture, Augustine did indeed …"Pick it up, read it; pick it up, read it". (8:12) Voraciously!

Some thirty-three years ago, as a young man (but already old in outlook, and having had enough of what this life offers) twenty-two years of age, I sat reading John 5:24 upon which my dominant emotion and thought was of SURPRISE. Surprised by the tense, the present tense, that one "could" know and possess, in THIS life, eternal life. I looked away and pondered, being completely SURPRISED. Looking back to the text (in the sovereignty of God my eyes, not returning to John 5:25, as one would suppose they would/should) my eyes fixated on John 5:28, whereupon in my "Living Bible" were the words, "DON"T BE SO SURPRISED"! THAT made me REALLY SURPRISED. Of course, my heart, mind, soul, and body were filled with joy! Like Augustine (10:27) I henceforth can ever "confess" before God; "Late it was that I loved you". It is therefore unashamedly, even with child-like faith, that I am happy to recommend (concerning the Scripture) to one and all; "Pick it up, read it; pick it up, read it". (8:12)

ESSAY 6: BEDE'S GREAT GREGORY

While our era of investigation this cycle spans nearly a thousand years of Church history, (AD 590-1517), this PSE concentrates largely on the rather short but certainly significant rule of Pope Gregory the Great, (at the opening of this era) as summarized by St. Bede. Written before AD731, Bede's account of the reign of Pope Gregory is replete with praise, thanksgiving, and appreciation for the one Bede credits with the veritable salvation of England. This is an era marked no doubt by the rise of Papal power, and the emergence (not only of Christian England) of Papal Nation States, but also the rise of scholasticism. It might perhaps be best to view the pontificate of Gregory as the kernel or catalyst of all of the above.

St. Bede (the venerable) wrote glowingly of Gregory! Interwoven throughout his assessment of Gregory is revealed his eternal gratitude for the zeal, longsuffering, humility, and even genius that Gregory brought as one sent (an apostle) to England. Without question, the salvation of England looms large over all that Bede writes concerning Gregory. Attributes and accomplishments particularly credited to Gregory include his ability to squelch a less than orthodox position held by Eutychus (then bishop of Constantinople) concerning the metaphysical attributes of the risen Christ. (Eutychus, btw, following his namesake from Acts 20, must indeed have slept through too much New Testament readings, or hit his head too hard on a fall!) In addition to "saving England" and "securing an Orthodox resurrection", Bede rightly credits Gregory with possessing and teaching about the "pastor's heart" needed by every good shepherd. Gregory wrote (Pastoral Care) of (reflecting an autobiographic sketch) how church leadership must possess and balance spiritual pursuits with earthly demands. The key for all of this (according to Gregory, revealed in his commentary on Job) was humility. Not at all disconnected to all of this is the legacy Gregory left. Along with significant liturgical improvements inclusive of music, (the Gregorian chants are named in his honor) Gregory saw to it that the Church (as opposed to the State) bore the burden of ministering charity in cultures of poverty. These endeavors reveal a heart for God, and a heart for God's people. There is little doubt but that all might rightly conclude Gregory to be what is often called "a GOOD Man". Our text, therefore (p.164), rightly characterizes this thus, " if goodness is the highest kind of greatness then the Church moved rightly in according him the title "Great". These last two areas of Gregory's work (music and charity) are why and how even Protestant reformers such as John Calvin could have such high regard and hold such esteemed assessments for a pope such as Gregory. This places Gregory in extremely rare territory.

St. Bede however, continues to praise Gregory for matters that perhaps are not so praise worthy; matters even that (in my estimation) make Gregory the Great perhaps Gregory the Not-So-Great. Under Gregory, expanded and official roles and rituals emerged with respect to Eucharistic Powers, Relics, Saints as Advocates, and (early release?) policies and procedures concerning Purgatory. These "mediatorial vehicles" were later even more formally advanced under the "pantheon" of Church endowments soon to become the "Treasury of Merit". Without question, these brought into question the special and exclusive role and place of Jesus the Christ. A perhaps unintended consequence (theologically) seems to point toward the possible entrance into eternal life in a way peripheral to and only marginally tangential to Jesus. All good intentions aside, to the casual reader, this humble pragmatist (Gregory) gave birth to a humanly "do-able" religion. Reading our textbook on Gregory, this writer was struck with the notion considering… was it possible that (surely unintended) Gregory's "do-able" religion "set the stage" for the later, (one generation) emergence of the most formidable "do-able" religion in all of history: Islam? By "set the stage", I do not at all imply ANY direct contact with or influence upon Mohammed, and it is not stated so as to attempt to wildly diminish the reputation of Gregory. It only strikes me oddly coincidental that these "do-able" religions emerged so chronologically close together. This exploration, an intriguing new thought for me, is way beyond the scope of this PSE. As a further aside in what I estimate to be yet another area of fascinating investigation; Gregory's novel understanding and assessment of Simon of Cyrene, potentially provides a treasure trove of psychological fodder for budding counselors concerning "projection" over his own embrace of the Papacy as punishment.

As important and significant as any other "fallout" of the "do-able" religion which developed and flourished under Gregory was the simple fact that it was the institution of the church who was the sole, authorized agent and administrator of such. This resulted in considerably increased institutional and papal power. This power translated into wealth, which spawned explosive growth in scholastic and architectural undertakings. Institutional bureaucracy and machinery was not "left behind" (sorry for that term usage!) in the advance. None of this is necessarily bad as there is little formidable credible opposition to the New Testament depiction of the Church as emerging in history as an institution visibly successful (Acts 15:16). That aside, (and as all men remain sinners) sinful excesses are always a risk. To these risks and temptations the Church often succumbs. Even though I remain a strong proponent of a strong institutional church and view Roman Catholics as (generally "weaker" ie. Romans 14) brothers in Christ, I do find more than a measure of divine irony wherein our textbook (page 199) revealed that (in the sovereignty of God) Canon Law emerged in "Bologna"!

No discussion of this era would be complete without the mention concerning the "Crusades". Spanning some two hundred years (1095-1291) involving several popes and seven major initiatives and assaults, the Crusades were as much the stuff of symbol and legend as they were of history. They have produced as much inspiration for Christian opponents and enemies, as they had for proponents. Perhaps well motivated, and as a "defensive" (re-capture) strategy, along with their certain (anti gnostic) claim that the "earth is the Lord's", the Crusades (though not largely successful) may not have been the colossal negative plight so often assigned by modern scholars. For every false step of ambition and assertion made a thousand years ago, there are several false steps of abdication and withdrawal today. For all the faultiness that may have been involved, the prospect of Christ embracing an advancing Crusader is far more palatable than the prospect of Christ embracing a retreating coward.

Rounding out this altogether too brief discussion on the Crusades is their use (by popes) as motivational vehicles. This is instructive for leadership today. The "age of the Crusades" smacks of the same dynamic of the modern day "Church building project". Used once, (somewhere) often highly successful in motivating the masses (congregation) it "comes of age" even as it faces diminishing returns. While, no doubt, both the Crusades and building projects may temporarily fill a "reason for being" void; the longer lasting, even eternal motivations of building the city of God on earth and the heavenly Jerusalem above far better signal the arrival of the age to come. With man, this is NOT "do-able". With God, all things are possible. Owning that would surely have made Gregory Great!

ESSAY 7: MENDICANTS/MENDERS/MENACES

In the absence of a single primary SOURCE document to analyze, the following is the presentation of a thesis statement attempting to explain and explore the conditions of the Church in the 13th and 14th centuries. The subject of the thesis is the emergence of forces acting upon the Church. To wit; there were the mendicants; those who were a menace to the Church; and those who were menders of the Church. (These came in the forms of, and as reformers, mystics, conciliatory spirits, and more.) All of these were necessary invitees, (most certainly not consciously desired as such) to the ecclesiastical scene, because, in the Church (according to our textbook p. 205) "pastoral care was a lost art". Our subject thesis therefore is:

"Lady Poverty" came into being as a result of the Church becoming so full of herself, not only by accumulating worldly wealth and power, but also by assuming to her (institutional) self the role of sole teat of Grace, that she came to resemble "Vanity Fair" far more than the Virgin Bride of Christ.

Addressing this detached, bloated, grossly idyllic institutional monster came the mendicants. Led by the likes of St. Francis of Assisi, men, women, and new movements grew which were closer in tune to, and aligned with, the "poor in Spirit". Some of these would prove to be a menace to the Church; others would prove to potentially be a part of Her mending. Mendicants of another sort, (if one could use such a term to describe a lowly "back to the Bible" teacher) also came into being. These found their voice not so much on an economic axis, but on a theological/ecclesiastical axis. There was, therefore, not only an impulse toward simpler and humbler material pursuits, but also toward simpler and humbler (more "Biblical") soteriological presentations. This latter pre-reformational impulse also consisted of those who would sometimes be a menace, others who would perhaps prove to sometimes be a mender; and then sometimes there were those who would even prove to be a blend of both.

Other "economic" mendicants consisted of the likes of Arnold of Brescia (peak ministry years: 1139-1155) and Peter Waldo (c. 1140-1218) of Lyons. More notable "ecclesiastical" mendicants were (later) men such as John Wyclif and John Hus. The artificial separate designation concerning "economic and ecclesiastical" is only presented to distinguish some of the NATURE of the push-back against "Vanity Fair" (Bunyan's later depiction). The reality was such that these separate designations may indeed be more artificially isolated than the impulses motivating any single one of the above mentioned reformers. Certainly though, the MATERIAL PROSPERITY of the institutional church was under redress, as was her MONOPOLY on the MACHINERY of dispensing GRACE. Following these same leaders and impulses came groups and organizations we know of as Franciscans, Dominicans, Waldensians, Cathari, Albigenses, Lollards, and Hussites. Adding to this "humble" de-centralizing impulse was a revival of a "mystic" impulse in the church. This is an impulse which had not entirely disappeared, yet became a growing reactionary force in the face of the wealth, power, formalism, and intellectual orientation of much of the scholastic movement. Some of scholasticism retained its spiritual/mystical edge, but not all. The monasteries themselves were a mixed bag. Men like Abelard were no small source of trouble. For many, their pride and their approaches, were just as problematic as their particular ideas and positions. Persons of great prominence in this realm (an appellation they would most certainly NOT appreciate) include: Bernard of Clairvaux and Julian of Norwich.

Not unexpectedly, arising out of these impulses, (especially the "economic" and "ecclesiastical" challenges) there came conflict. Even in mythology… "The Empire Strikes Back"! So too in history! The clashes that emerged came in both civil and in barbaric fashion. Prominently among them are the following:

The councils (Lateran/Constance/Basel) formed the basis of what is called the "Conciliar Movement" represent a type of the former, while the Inquisition typifies the latter. While the term "inquisition" has come to epitomize jurisprudential INJUSTICE, we still tend to have something of a sanitized view of what went on. We tend to think of it as limited to an "unfair" debate, interview, or accusation. Perhaps mean-spirited. The scene at the close of "Braveheart" should be a potent corrective to whatever misunderstandings we might have concerning the depths of depravity, even among the so-called righteous powers that be. Each of these (the civil and barbaric responses) however, further enraged and emboldened the reformers. Likewise, institutional and papal power grew and consolidated during and under these "remedies". Instead of these impulses being seen, received and embraced as corrections from brothers, they were viewed as threats from outsiders, enemies, even apostates. (Imagine, if they had been received as David modeled; "Let the righteous smite me; it shall be a kindness. And let him reprove me; it shall be an excellent oil, which shall not break my head…" Ps. 141:5.) Failing that, the concept of the HERETIC came into fuller view. Not at all that they WERE outsiders, enemies, or apostates. (Though God knows the secrets of every heart.) They were, in fact, fellow "Christians" marked as such by Baptism. Heresy in that medieval period (as our textbook, p. 206; so well portrays) was not so much marked (as it might be today) by any particularized personally held belief, as it was the challenge to "ecclesiastical correctness" and authority. Whereas today we might speak of matters being "PC" that being politically correct; they would resonate more with everyone required to be "EC" as in ecclesiastically correct. Like commensurate with "treason" of today, "heresy" was of yesterday; complete with the corresponding sanctions!

Though it would not be formalized (in hindsight) until 1517, the Reformation was indeed percolating. As our textbook so masterfully communicates (p. 232) there was a season, "primed" for reform from within. But alas, it was not then to be. The shattering of Christendom was the soon to be result.

Perhaps, just perhaps as a new season and cycle emerges, even with a new FRANCIS, (Signaling a new round of mendicants?) the time has come where and when "Vanity Fair" will repent and reform and even be reunited with Her estranged, "separated" brothers, coming one step closer to fulfilling Her role as the Virgin Bride of Christ She ontologically is, was called to be, and one day visibly will be.

ESSAY 8: REFORMATIONAL TENETS & TEMPERAMENTS

Separating men (and women for that matter) from the movements they are leading and/or are caught up in, is always a delicate and tenuous task. As we herein explore the Lutheran, Anabaptist, and Reformed expressions of Protestantism, no doubt, names will be mentioned. Yet determining exactly how closely those persons should be associated with the movements or theologies (often named after them) can often be considerably debated if not problematic. For example… how close is Lutheranism (then and/or now) to be identified with Martin Luther? Perhaps in some aspects, considerably so, in other aspects, would even Luther own up to what is expressed in his name? Nevertheless, the exploration of the various religious tenets of the Reformation is aided by the exploration of the "players". ("Players" is purposely employed to appreciate the way Shelley demonstrated Calvin as "thrust into the game.) Rounding out this introduction, driving home this previous point powerfully is the fact that in recent years there have been those who posit that "there is no such thing as history… there is only biography." (Attributed to who else, but Winston Churchill!) Such is the strength and pull of the human element on that which we call history! Alas, how and where can/does one separate Johannes Gutenberg from the printing press?

According to Shelley, the Protestant Reformation indeed answered in a new way four basic questions. They are: 1) How is a person saved? 2) Where does religious authority lie? 3) What is the Church? 4) What is the essence of Christian Living? Though not nearly the full story of Luther or Lutheranism, Shelley credits Luther as providing answers to these four questions as those which "to this day any classical description of Protestantism must echo…", as "central truths." (p. 246) to wit, Luther posited that a person is saved not by works but by faith alone. Further, religious authority did not lie in the visible institution called the Roman Church but in the Word of God found in the Bible. Thirdly, Luther saw the whole community of Christian believers as the Church – even advocating for the priesthood of all believers. Finally, further developed by the magisterial reformers, Luther taught that the essence of Christian living was to serve God in any useful calling. A veritable doctrine of divine callings emerged with those reformers who would later give voice that the chief end of man was (and is) to glorify God and enjoy Him forever.

As the above indicates, whereas Shelley views the above as that which is uniformly Protestant, our readings and research reveals that the reformers were far from a monolithic group; and their tenets were as diverse as their temperaments.

Following up the Pre-Reformational urgings and thrusts from the likes of Waldo, Hus, and Wyclif, Luther emerges as a central key figure. A seminal moment no doubt, was October 31, 1517, when Luther posted his now famous 95 Theses. Almost equally important, by the summer of 1520 when Luther rejected the Papal bull to repent, it was clear that this "Wild Boar" (as Leo X called him) had invaded God's vineyard. Talk about "game on!" And what a "perfect storm" this "game on" was! (It should be interjected here… that it is most debatable that Luther ever originally meant to "leave", much less "destroy" the Church. Their response however, drew battle lines from which mortals rarely retreat.) For sure, the theological issues as cited (earlier) in those four questions loomed large, but so did the tangential issues of money, (Indulgences…ala: John Tetzel, going to Rome instead of staying in Germany) and power, (Nationalism on the rise). Then, of course, there was institutional power vis-à-vis individual power. The Renaissance clearly played no small role in impacting the two greatest cultural structures and strictures of the age: the feudal Lords and the medieval Prelates. Not at all lost in this institutional shake-up was Luther's own discovery (along with his ex- priestly contemporaries) of the adjustments needed to finding "a pair of pigtails on the pillow which were not there before". (p. 243)

Following Luther and much to his dismay came the Anabaptists. These were the "radical reformers". Comprised of the likes of Grebal and Manz, and (sadly) representative as "forerunners of practically all modern Protestants" (p. 248), Anabaptists embrace a veritable New Testament only expression of the faith with Christendom giving way to Christianity. For the Anabaptist, salvation would be marked by a decisionism borne of personal choice, with next to no authority save that of being true to oneself and their personal interpretations of (largely New Testament) Scripture. As for the Church, she still could exist in some form as an organism but was mostly invisible (pun intended) as an institution. Luther would later weep over the antinomianism (lawless) nature of Anabaptist theology (largely often cleverly concealed today in, of all things; legalism). Space does not allow for a full depiction of the defeatism, dualism, destruction and despotism born of the Anabaptist Radicals. Herman Munster of the Adams family is a creature in far greater conformity to Christ than the likes of those emerging from Munster. All (possible) good intentions aside, the truncated WORD (New Testament only) embraced by the Anabaptists with its political pacifism and economic socialism leads to love that is a lie, and reveals more a Buddhist "inlook" rather than a Christian "outlook". It is indeed my hope that Anabaptist fortunes do not rise and that to whatever degree they may be "Pioneers of Modern Christianity" (as Shelley p. 253), God would save us from such monstrous modernity.

Brighter visions beamed afar as a result of the comprehensive covenant theology as advanced by the likes of John Calvin. God's glory, purposes, sovereignty, and Lordship were all hallmarks of Reformed thinking. As all men are sinners, the Magisterial Reformers could have handled many matters utilizing more light than heat... an assessment Michael Servetus would certainly have affirmed! Like Lutheranism and Martin Luther, Calvinism, (rightly or wrongly/ for good or ill) has become associated with John Calvin. As complex as Calvinism can sometimes be characterized as, Calvin ever and always wanted men to let God be God! This meant that the Christian ought to simply participate in the (two) Sacraments, and live an upright moral life consistent with a public profession of faith, (p. 261). For Calvin, salvation came by way of God's sovereign predestinating and electing grace. While the Anabaptist might say "God rocks", Calvinists say "God rules". His Word (66 books, not 27+) therefore is the final authority and the standard for conducting the whole of one's life. God's Church therefore, was the bride of Christ, complete with delegated maternal authority to direct and nurture the saints. Significantly profound was John Knox's evaluation of the implementation of Calvinism at Geneva as "the most perfect school of Christ that ever was on earth … ." (p. 260).

The Reformation era would not be complete without at least a cursory mention of the Church of England. Though outside the parameters of this PSE, Shelley magnificently captures (perhaps even unintentionally) the initial significance of the English Reformation (with the fullness of semantic range) by citing that it began (p. 264) in the "AFFAIRS of State".

ESSAY 9: WINTHROP'S MODEL OF CHRISTIAN CHARITY

Writing with the requisite skill and precision of the lawyer he was, which the Christian Covenant Theology of that era so readily produced, John Winthrop, in 1630, aboard the Arbella, penned his Model of Christian Charity. Beginning and ending with God and His Word, this document traces the hopes, aspirations, and duties Winthrop desired a community of Puritan transplants from the Old World to the New World to embrace. Winthrop saw all men in their varying stations and conditions as under God and for His Glorie (the Middle English spelling sort of grows on you!). Among these stations and conditions were the rich and the poor, the dignified and the mean, and also the regenerate and the "strangers". Said stations and conditions themselves revealed the wise council and order of God, and provided the means and opportunity for the further manifestation of His power and Spirit in unifying them. Such stations and conditions were the veritable "facts of life" of the 17th century. Winthrop would have been very comfortable with (he is even revealing of) language used (during that generation) in countless other formal documents (many of a catechetical fashion) citing: the preserving the honor, performing the duties, and forbidding the neglect of that which belongs to everyone in their several places and relations, as (get this) superiors, inferiors, or equals. Imagine that; superiors, inferiors, or equals! The egalitarianism of our day would fly in the face as an outrage before those of Winthrop's day.

Far from bringing shame or embarrassment (which might be the case today), this social structure was viewed as honorable and implicitly Christian. The regulation of this social structure would also bring additional glory to God through the codification and implementation of His Laws and principles for governing all of these affairs (and facts) of life. Informing and directing the community would be the Biblical principle of LOVE as thee over-riding (umbrella) motive. Of course, Biblically speaking, love is never merely a motive or a mere emotion. Love requires action. The "bonds of brotherly affection" would govern ("Do good") the community with discernment (Gal. 6:10) concerning "brethren" and "strangers". Even "enemies" would be loved (Mt. 5:44), for whereas the law of nature gives no guidance for such, the Law of Christ in the Gospel does plentifully supply. Thus, in this "doing unto all others", the Golden Rule (Mt. 7:12) is referenced. Love, of course and by necessity, would recognize the varying seasons and occasions upon which greater charity ought to be exercised. Times of profound peril would necessitate equally profound acts of love, mercy, sacrifice and service. Winthrop strongly cited the "BODY" imagery of 1 Corinthians 12 as representative of the community members' inter-relationship, inter-action, inter-dependency, and co-honor. From Ephesians 4:16, Winthrop views the community as "knit" together, and gleaning from 1 John 4, Winthrop repeatedly cites that "love is the bond of perfection".

Along with love, the Model of Christian Charity cites Scriptural authority and direction for regulating (even requiring) matters such as GIVING, LENDING, and FORGIVING. Extensively referenced is the motive behind, and the blessings attendant upon those practicing the "true" fasts and Sabbaths of Isaiah 58. These of course never divorced the service of the social from (and in) the pursuit of the spiritual. In addition and not at all lost on Winthrop were the themes of MERCY and JUSTICE. Invoking the Prophet Micah (6:8), Winthrop implores not only for their present, but also for their posterity, that they "do justly" and "love mercy". Though not explicitly or extensively developed, INDUSTRY is engendered and encouraged; "and he is worse than an infidel that provideth not for his own" (1 Tim 5:8). Combined with the fact that sloth is specifically referenced as a vice, it is clear that a person's industry and labor were viewed as a virtue and a blessing for and to himself and others. Though it may seem otherwise, the Protestant work ethic is not nearly as far in our rear view mirror as the dinosaur.

Perhaps not so much a Biblical principle, COVENANT as a Biblical paradigm is unquestionably behind and advanced in Winthrop's Model of Christian Charity. Toward the close of the document the word "covenant" and its concepts are repeatedly employed. Sanctions (blessings and curses) are cited as consequences concerning faithfulness (success) or unfaithfulness, (failure). The latter was viewed as a spiritual shipwreck far more to be avoided, and far deadlier than the very real threat of that sort of actual calamity. As the eyes of all people were upon them, they were indeed as a "city upon a hill". Further illustrative of covenantal thinking is the "telos" which closes out the document. Winthrop extends not so much a good-bye, but a "fare-well" charge citing Deuteronomy 30. Therein he saw the Puritan purpose, (telos) and destination, (telos):

"Therefore, let us choose life that we and our seed may live by obeying His voice and cleaving to Him, for He is our life and our prosperity."

How did reality coincide with the ideal set forth by Winthrop? First, the particular "perils" of the new world were appreciably greater than most at that time envisioned. The harshness of climate alone brought challenges considerably unbearable. Today we would call it a logistical nightmare. Second, while covenant theology allows for theocracy, Winthrop seemed to make no provision for any daylight between the civil and the ecclesiastical forms of government. Third, the spacious land mass made for a ready exodus for any and all who were discontent: not to mention ample space for banishment! Fourth, it should be noted that all men are sinners, and it is the condition of the heart rather than the color of the skin that tends to make and reveal one as a savage. As Chesterton has quipped, "There are an infinity of angles at which man falls; yet one, at which man stands". This is cited because where and how (and to the degree), the Puritans failed – they did so by their vices. Their failure to follow the dictates of Winthrop's document was far more instrumental to their demise (and limited significance) than their keeping of it. That one angle by which a man (and society) stands is "In Christ", and that, in word and in deed.

Contrariwise, the following ought to be remembered. Amazingly, (miraculously?) they did survive! Secondly, the nation born out of the likes of the Puritans has singularly been (by far) the greatest blessing to all the peoples of all nations in the history of the world. Thirdly, no nation has rivaled that nation concerning the increase of peace and prosperity. Finally, warts and all, (which are considerable and for all to see) while some like to close their eyes to this truth; In His sanctioning of that nation with tremendous blessings and severe judgments, corresponding to faithfulness and the lack thereof, (the paradigm and principles outlined in Winthrop's Model of Christian Charity) God has indeed set that land as a "city upon a hill". With the whole world STILL watching, will She shine or will the lights go out?

Meanwhile, not to be confused or equated with THAT city, the New Jerusalem shines on!

ESSAY 10: THE FEMALE MORAL REFORM SOCIETY

Our PSE this cycle is an analysis of the Female Moral Reform Society, one of many evangelical voluntary associations formed in the mid nineteenth century. Cause and effect must always be addressed carefully, yet it is intriguing if not telling that our assignment page opens with this clause, "In the wake of the Second Great Awakening". Perhaps, it is owing to a Godly zeal resultant of that "revival" that the FMRS was formed. Perhaps, however, it is also partly owing to that "revival" as being a contributory cause of the conditions created which begged and demanded the emergence of such a group. Perhaps a bit of both. While no one can doubt the deplorable moral conditions of that era, there is plenty of room for speculation concerning origin and cause. The greater part of this PSE will be an analysis of the FMRS, complete with nothing other than the highest regard for the zeal and motivations of those who participated. Yet first, what of the factors that precipitated such a calamitous environment? As a lifelong and present day resident of (Troy) the "eastern front" of the "burnt-over district", (Troy to Buffalo) of New York, in which every green thing was scorched and withered during the "revivals" (in Troy, 1826-1827) of Finney et al; Warfield's assessment rings true: This was a "Pelagian revival" with Finney himself imbibing heavily and being himself drunk on the "New Divinity" and its "new measures". (BTW, it was profound and ironic to learn in my own research that it was none other than Mrs. (Lydia) Finney who played a major leadership role in establishing the FMRS.) On the heels of those "revivals" upstate New York became a vast spiritual wasteland. Churches and pastorates were destroyed. Charitable works and Christian love ceased. It was reported that even the Bible was set aside, and "feelings" became a substitute for duty. The older-schooled Christendom and Calvinistic features were overwhelmed. Remini has written: "As the revivals grew and intensified in enthusiasm, they frequently ended in orgies of excess…". Orgies of excess of every kind. In the vacuum generated by this further destruction of Christendom, as existing authorities collapsed, anarchy reigned. Excellent resources for this era include Warfield's "Studies in Perfectionism" and North's "Crossed Fingers: How the Liberals Captured the Presbyterian Church". The point of this cursory review and history is that many of the social conditions encountered and combatted by the FMRS are the very ones (perhaps) generated and/or exacerbated by the "revival" itself. None of this is to say that there were not many, perhaps even thousands of genuine conversions. Nor is it to say that the revival was not responsible for generating the zeal to combat these conditions. Yet inside and outside the church, "the times they were a changing". Everything from "free-sex" to "sex-free" groups emerged. This is where and when the spiritualist Fox sisters emerged, as did Mormonism. Out of this era came Welch's grape juice, Kellogg's corn flakes and Graham's crackers to reduce man's carnal "beastly" instincts. Are you kidding me? Indeed what better time for a perfectionistic instinct to emerge than a time of reckless sinful indulgence.

Such is the environment into which FMRS was born. Regardless of the origin of the conditions, the founders of the FMRS (as every Christian must) dealt with the facts as found on the ground. Attempting to follow in the footsteps and continue the lifework of Rev. John McDowell, FMRS motivated by compassion (which is always a good motivation), sought to help and reclaim women as the abuse victims of a wildly "licentious" (not to mention still too patriarchal for many tastes) culture. Largely following the model of (and collaborating with) the temperance movement, FMRS became a public relations/opinion association as much as anything else. Our terminology today is "advocacy group".

Initial impressions of this document reveal founders who are genuinely concerned and convicted about the moral state of the country. There is almost a naiveté revealed in their "shock" and seemingly newfound alert and awareness as to the sinfulness (particularly sexual) of man (and particularly men). Theirs is a "pull out all the stops" approach toward a greater commitment to the seventh commandment. Particularly addressed is the need to combat the "double standard" by which men were (are?) often excused, (sometimes admired) for that which any (and every) woman is accused (and even trashed). For sure, the document reads a bit like a part of the playbook in "the battle of the sexes". Men certainly come out on the losing side, being portrayed as the "dirt bags" they are in Adam. Without completely exonerating all women, the document certainly portrays men as perpetrators and women as victims. He is the hunter, she is the hunted, even though the Bible reveals that these roles may sometimes be reversed (Proverbs 7:12&13). Through the FMRS, women were enjoined to defend themselves, respect themselves, and at every point to expose and repudiate the above mentioned "double standard". That sinful men might be on the same receiving end of "disgrace" that all sinful people deserve seems a notable goal of FMRS. The desired effect hoped for was that men would "cease and desist" from their sexual sin and exploitations. In addition to the NYC home base, missionary ventures ensued soliciting and distributing benevolences from and toward the major cities, (Boston, Providence, Albany, Philadelphia, and Baltimore) as a part of their operation. Also of significance, rightly educating the next generation, the children, by "stirring up parents, teachers, and ministers" as to the importance of these matters was deemed most critical. The neglect of said instruction is cited as to have played a complicit role in the deplorable then-present state.

Believing as I do, in Christendom far more than in Christianity, social and political (I cannot separate) activism is a component of what we do as Christians. Of course, our primary focus is spiritual and is on the King. Yet, I see no Biblical warrant (or allowance) for failing to address and focus on the social as He has commanded, for this, His Kingdom. If and as I am to pray, "Thy will be done on earth, as it is in heaven", I must act accordingly. The type of work done by the FMRS is noble and honorable. More than that, it is necessary and Biblical. I tend to think that the need for this type of work is exacerbated by the evisceration of robust Christendom and the subsequent moral authority void that follows. I believe it to be unfortunate that (as so many, even Christians, gleefully rejoice in the continuing dismantling of whatever is left of Christendom,) we are left with the scattered hodge-podge of a myriad (exceeding ten thousand times ten thousand and thousands of thousands!) of groups like FMRS endeavoring to do the very work their Christendom forebearers had done, or at least were trying to do. I'm not sure (all efforts and motivations aside) that the results of the former (groups like FMRS) are any better or different than the results of the latter (those Christendom forebearers). Nevertheless, seeing as we ought, the facts on the ground as they are, we too must pray, think and act.

In the absence of a robust Christendom, advocacy groups such as FMRS have a place and calling. Surely God uses, blesses, and smiles upon such good works. Yet, the lifecycle and lifespan of such groups typically includes a fate whereby they become beholden to, and (eventually) an arm of, the secular State. Much better would be a fate of one nurtured under, and directed by, the arms of their Spiritual Mother.

ESSAY 11: MLK JR.'S: PAUL'S LETTER TO AMERICAN CHRISTIANS

Two score and five years ago, I sat as a ten year old boy glued to our "black and white" TV set. On April 4th, 1968 one presented as a national hero was assassinated. All people mourned. The ensuing years have revealed much concerning the life and work of Dr. Martin Luther King Jr. Much has been made of his character and connections. In the minds and hearts of some there hardly could be a more saintly figure. For others, modernity hardly knows one who was a greater hypocrite or commie-fascist. Yet it might best be said that there scarcely has been a greater rhetorician. Years earlier, in 1963, on the national mall his "I Have A Dream" speech captured the hearts, minds, and imaginations of the nation, if not the world. In the mere hours before April 4, 1968, MLK Jr. gave an impassioned speech entitled "I Have Been To The Mountaintop". Each of these represented magnificent rhetoric, and each of these were theme-based concerning justice. The same is true for the speech and document analyzed herein, Martin Luther King Jr.'s: "Paul's Letter To American Christians", first delivered November 4th, 1956 at the Dexter Avenue Baptist Church in Montgomery, Alabama. Though King tries to mimic St. Paul, perhaps his greater aim (of which he equally falls short) is to be an Amos: "Let judgment roll down as waters, and righteousness as a mighty stream".

While King says many noteworthy and valuable things, he is no St. Paul. The Apostle Paul would never conclude, as King does, that moral ascendency might be commensurate with scientific and technological progress, improvements and advances. St Paul knew that sin was far more deep-seated and individually animated than that which might be remedied by mere human endeavors and achievements (however impressive or exalted). Nor could sin be remedied by mere prohibition. St. Paul would never have railed against "economic systems" be they capitalism or communism. (He certainly had the chance to do so considering the rampant slavery of his day, and certainly the American landscape was a veritable economic picnic if not paradise compared to that of the pagan Roman Empire.) King is to be credited and commended for (at least) referencing the economic injustices he saw as owing to a "misuse" of capitalism. Intentionally or otherwise, King's rhetorical desire to "better distribute wealth" fans and flames the support of those who would demand such by political coercion rather than by the Gospel means which encourages moral persuasion. There is a world of difference between moral persuasion and political coercion! While gross materialism is a problem of every age, invoking the rebuke of King and Paul alike, I'm not as sure as King was that Paul saw God as never intending an economic gap (however sizeable) between the masses. God has said that the poor, you will always have with you. (This is all reminiscent of the argument that goes… if money is such a big problem, why is there such an interest in seeing it passed about so broadly?) St. Paul's greater concern (in contrast to King, citing not external public circumstances but inward private conditions) seemed to be that one live honorably, contentedly, thankfully and in a sanctified manner "in" the station you find yourself. If and as one may advance, do so; if not, then abide! Perhaps more telling (revealing) of King's political/economic philosophy was his 1965 "Playboy" interview (of all places!) wherein he advanced what we call today the concept of "reparations" for past injustices.

Part of what King does well is revealing the folly and futility of "democracy" as a moral barometer. He would do better to recognize that it (democracy) is of no better use politically. Voltaire notwithstanding, the "voice of the people" might not be the voice of God morally or politically.

King gets high marks for combatting violence, sectarianism, and segregation. Among his comments decrying violence and the need to resist the temptation to fall into it, there is one that is most prophetic. He spoke "if you succumb to the temptation of using violence in your struggle, UNBORN GENERATIONS will be the recipient of a long and desolate night of bitterness, and your chief legacy to the future will be an endless reign of meaningless chaos". How true concerning the violence succumbed to resulting in (and following from) the 1973 Roe v. Wade decision! What an impact on those very same UNBORN GENERATIONS!

With respect to sectarianism, King is an equal opportunity critic of both Protestant and Catholic expressions of the Faith. Three cheers!!!

Segregationist matters are a little more complex. To the degree they are (as they largely were) motivated racially, they are to be condemned. This cannot be stated too strongly. On the other hand, to the degree that "birds of a feather, (simply prefer) choose to flock together" (voluntarily), I see no real sin. It may remain to one's own hurt and stunting of growth that they may lack awareness and appreciation of others, yet, even God, in His eternal Kingdom is glorified by being worshipped by diverse groups in their diversity; every nation, tribe and tongue. Is there not a harmony and a beautiful stereophonic fullness that is lost when all becomes a monolithic, androgynous, univocal melody?

A greater contribution of Kings' PLAC is that he echoes St. Paul's reminder that we indeed have a dual citizenship with a primary allegiance above. Christians of every generation are called upon and challenged with issues confronting our allegiances. "Evil" segregation was one. Continued racism remains one! Among the other civil/social/economic injustices of today remain the plight (annihilation) of the unborn, the sexual trafficking (particularly youthful Asian) of females, and the corruption (manipulation/devaluation) of currency with its complicit use of dishonorable weights and measures. Everyone should know by now that capitalism without a Christian foundation is no superior economic model to any other. Hence our "issues" are moral, as they ever were, and ever will be.

Where King is most consistent with St. Paul is his insistence on love as the motivating factor in all of the above. Here his rhetoric soars. Indeed, without love, life becomes a "meaningless drama" and love is, even at the least: "the heartbeat of the moral cosmos". All people do well to heed that love is indeed a prerequisite as one hopes, aspires and expects to "matriculate into the University of Eternal Life".

As I close out this analysis of Dr. King's PLAC, it is my hope that it is owing to a transcriber's error and not Dr. King's sentiment that in the closing doxology wherein (repeatedly) the "him" referenced as God, is disrespectfully presented beginning with the lower case "h". I would like to think of MLK Jr. as bowing to the King as the King. Only heaven knows!

All in all, as per Dr. King's own opening request, I will attribute "to his lack of complete objectivity" rather than a "lack of St. Paul's clarity", the fact that this letter did largely sound "strangely Kingian" instead of "Paulinian". Better yet would it have been, to let Paul be Paul, and let the King be King! Sorry Elvis, you are not even on the radar screen!

APPENDIX: "PRECIOUS SONS OF ZION"
ERIC LIDDELL AND DEITRICH BONHOEFFER:
GUIDING LIGHTS FOR THE NEW DARK AGES

This paper will trace their biographies, including the discipline, dedication, and self-denial that made them such prominent persons in athletics and academia respectively. It will apply these character traits to their ability to engage their greatest calling; as lambs led to the slaughter in the face of the anti-christian totalitarianism of their day, and their special (even life-sacrificing) roles. In times of calamity and collapse, they answer the question... "If the foundations be destroyed, what can the righteous do?" (Psalm 11:3) Areas of application and relation to the church include the place and role of the would be idols of "Muscular Christianity" (sports), and intellectual credentialism (doctrinal snobbery), and how the Christian can overcome them. "Precious Sons" also inspires toward how contemporary Christians might ready themselves for the new dark ages, as our world hurdles toward the latest manifestation of anti-Christian totalitarianism.

Introduction

Among those "of whom the world was not worthy" (Hebrews 11:38) stands a myriad of saints belonging to the "Faith Hall of Fame". "Precious sons, comparable to fine gold", who are treated as mere earthen vessels (Lamentations 4:2), the trial of whose faith has been found to be more precious than gold, (1 Peter 1:7) are known in every generation. The prophet Jeremiah himself was among them and knew them. Over 2500 years ago he lamented over their demise and destruction at the hands of the Babylonians. Such is the witness and testimony of the lives (and deaths) of Eric Liddell and Dietrich Bonhoeffer. Moreover, like St. Peter before them, they went a way they "would not". A way not of their choosing, but a way they could have avoided. Yet in submission to their Lord, like St. Peter, they fully surrendered. They possessed a strong testimony of Jesus "and, they loved not their lives unto the death" (Rev.12:11).

Born just a few years apart, Liddell, (1902) and Bonhoeffer (1906), and dying (in the midst and mist of the fog that all war is) mere days apart in 1945, these giants of the faith lived a veritable parallel existence. While no evidence has been found that they ever met, and it seems unlikely that they even knew of each other, Liddell and Bonhoeffer were united in their commitment to Christ and the sacrificially fleshing out of His commandments, especially the notation recorded by St. John; "greater love has no man than this, that a man lay down his life for his friends", (John 15:13).

Liddell and Bonhoeffer each were "golden boys" of sorts: Liddell as a gold medal recipient at the Paris Olympics in 1924, and Bonhoeffer as one whose name has become a synonym for Christian Ethics summarized in the "Golden Rule" of St. Matthew's Gospel. Whatever else might be said of Liddell and Bonhoeffer, they are among those having earned and deserving of a golden crown of glory. While earthly acclaim no doubt has (and is itself) a reward and writers such as Tom Brokaw list notables and not-so notables in works such as "The Greatest Generation", heavenly acclaim and registry in the Lamb's Book of Life is the highest reward and honor.

Celebrity and Caricature

During their short lives, while Bonhoeffer knew limited notoriety outside of academia, Liddell (despite Olympic Gold) knew next to none. Each however has been the recipient of much notoriety post-humously. In 1980, the major motion picture release of "Chariots of Fire" exploded on the world-wide scene making Eric Liddell a virtual household name. A fascinating analysis of that film by Cashmore paints it as "most profitably understood as an invigorating sermon for the 1980's rather than a literal or authentic record of the 1920's".[1] This highly recommended article dissects and then describes the movie as largely fictional, fabricated from the socio-economic features of the Margaret Thatcher era, and importing the sports crazed characteristics of earlier and latter generations. While the skeletal aspects of Liddell's Olympic achievement are historical and factual, much of "Chariots of Fire" is a "fanciful moralizing", a "mythic meditation", a "faultless hagiography", and a "curate's egg".[2] Yet, it is from "Chariots of Fire" that most people know of Eric Liddell's life and work. Renewed and expanded (outside of academia) celebrity for Bonhoeffer has come even more recently. In 2010, Eric Metaxas ignited an explosion of interest and exploration into the life, mind, and times (not to mention theology) of Bonhoeffer. His block buster book, "Bonhoeffer: Pastor, Prophet, Martyr, Spy" has not only been credited for reintroducing Bonheoffer to a new generation, but criticized for "hijacking Bonhoeffer".[3] As a result of the frenzy and firestorm created in the wake of Metaxas' book, a host of re-examination of Bonhoeffer's theology has emerged including notable pieces by Weikhart[4] and Barnett.[5] Bonhoeffer is also now featured further in the blog world with none other than "Dr. Reluctant" discussing "what to think about, and what to do about Dietrich Bonhoeffer".[6]

Background and Biography

Owing consciously or otherwise to the blessings of Christendom, the peace and prosperity of the homes and families that produced Liddell and Bonhoeffer demonstrates indeed that (generally) good trees bring forth good fruit and that the fruit (generally) doesn't fall far from the tree. Each of these "precious sons" was the product of intact homes with noble heritage. Their fathers were notable, successful men and solid role models. Credited to their mothers are fruitful homes whose atmosphere was fragranced by love, nurture, music, and learning, as well as a sense of calling and duty.

Into an overtly Christian home of missionary parents came Eric Liddell in 1902. Born on the mission field

---

[1] Ellis Cashmore, *Chariots of Fire: Bigotry, Manhood and Moral Certitude in an Age of Individualism. Sports in Society: Cultures, Commerce, Media, Politics*, 11:2-3; 159-173. (2008). P. 172
[2] Ibid. P. 171
[3] Clifford Green, *Hijacking Bonhoeffer*. The Christian Century, October 5, 2010. The Thoughtful Christian.com
[4] Richard, Weikhart, *"Metaxas's Counterfeit Bonhoeffer: An Evangelical Critique"*. California State University, Stanislaus.
[5] Victoria Barnett. *Bonhoeffer. A Biography*, Philadelphia: Fortress Press, 2000.
[6] Paul Martin, Henebury, *Dr. Reluctant: "What to think about Dietrich Bonhoeffer"?* WordPress.com

in Tientsin, China, of Scottish heritage, Liddell was schooled in Edinburgh.[7] Liddell not only excelled at school, earning a Bachelor's degree in chemistry, physics and mathematics,[8] but also excelled in sports. His Sabbatarian convictions stirred controversy but his critics were silenced as he ran for gold in the 1924 Olympic Games in Paris.[9] Attributed to this circumstance is the Scriptural promise, "...them that honor Me, I will honor..." (1Sam.2:30). The level of discipline and conviction needed to accomplish all of the above speaks for itself. After the Olympics, Liddell taught at the Anglo-American Chinese College where his call to missions was confirmed, and he applied to the London Missionary Society[10] for theological training. Being the worker and servant he was, with constant interruption due to speaking engagement demand, he wasn't formally ordained until 1938.[11] Called to his side as helpmeet came Florence MacKenzie from a fellow missionary family in Tientsin out of Canada.[12] On her eighteenth birthday, they promised their secret engagement intentions one to another.[13] It was almost five years later when they married on Tuesday, March 27, 1934.[14] Speaking of character building (and the displaying of) discipline and restraint!! Over the years, born to the Liddell's were three daughters. A long life was not in God's plan for Eric. He would by dead by 1945 after two trying years of separation from Flo and family, (who for safety returned to Canada) and forced internment in Weihsien Camp by the Japanese occupying army.[15] While the camp provisions were far less than ideal, it is believed that his cause of death was a brain tumor or hemorrhage which even the finest of medical care, (which he did not receive) could not have successfully dealt with nor prevented.[16]

If Liddell's life may be viewed as one caught up in the crosswinds of political change and calamity, Bonhoeffer's was caught up in a whirlwind! Yet all began in great calm. Born to Karl and Paula Bonhoeffer in 1906 was Dietrich, their fourth and youngest son just ten minutes before his twin sister, Sabine.[17] Eberhard Bethge elaborates on the earlier made remarks concerning heritage:

> "The rich world of his ancestors set the standards for Dietrich Bonhoeffer's own life.
> It gave him a certainty of judgment and manner that cannot be acquired in a single
> generation. He grew up in a family that believed the essence of learning lay not in a formal education
> but in the deeply rooted obligation to be guardians of a great historical heritage and intellectual
> tradition."[18]

More nominally Christian than the more radically professing Liddells, the Bonhoeffers were no less heirs of the blessings of Christendom. Father Karl was an accomplished professional who held the university chair in psychiatry and neurology,[19] while mom, no less accomplished as a teacher, opted to home-school the children.[20] The Germany of Dietrich's youth was still largely Lutheran, but the Bonhoeffer's were influenced

---

[7] J.D. Douglas, ed. *The New International Dictionary of the* Christian *Church,* Grand Rapids: Zondervan, 1974. P.595
[8] Scott A., Moreau, *Evangelical Dictionary of World Missions.* Grand Rapids: Baker Books, 2000. P.577
[9] Ibid. P. 577
[10] Ibid. P.577
[11] Scott A., Moreau, *Evangelical Dictionary of World Missions.* Grand Rapids: Baker Books, 2000. P.577
[12] David, McCasland. *Eric Liddell, Pure Gold.* Grand Rapids: Discovery House, 2001. P.135
[13] Ibid. P.147
[14] Ibid. P.179
[15] Ibid. P.251ff
[16] Ibid. P.281
[17] Eric, Metaxas . *Bonhoeffer: Pastor, Prophet, Martyr, Spy.* Nashville: Thomas Nelson, 2010. P. 8
[18] Ibid. P.5
[19] Ibid. P.8
[20] Ibid. P.9

25

by the impact of Count Zinzendorf of the eighteenth century and thereby exhibited a highly devotional, yet homespun embrace of the faith.[21] Early commitment to the Scripture became a life-long habit. While parents and siblings alike were impressed with Dietrich's talent in music and training in the sciences, they were not so sure that his choice of becoming a theologian was the best for him.[22] Yet thus began a most impressive academic, intellectual and theological career. Bonhoeffer also was travelling in a spiritual direction opposite that of his nation. Precisely where any particular point of conversion may lie is anyone's guess (and many have). Suffice it to say that Dietrich was increasingly living in a conscious state of being called by God, and concerned that his was a walk worthy of that calling. His call and teaching of "ethics" meant things in Germany by the mid 1930's. Hitler's Nazism was taking effect with Bonhoeffer convinced that the time had come for Germans and Jews to "stand together".[23] Increasingly and politically Bonhoeffer emerged as an important voice and figure in identifying the evil in, and opposing Hitler. By 1939, Bonhoeffer, (though now a world renowned academic/theological figure and tempted to wait out the plight of Germany in the US) decided to cast his lot with and in Germany.[24] In ways both overt and covert, Bonhoeffer spent the next several years opposing the Gestapo, Hitler, and the Third Reich. In all of these actions and choices, Bonhoeffer displays the courage, selflessness, and costly discipleship for which he has, in a renewed way become famous.[25]

Bonheoffer's final road to Calvary began with his imprisonment in 1943 and his execution, (hanging) in 1945. In a sermon preached while pastoring in London, Bonhoeffer said this about death;

> *"No one has yet believed in God and the kingdom of God, no one has yet heard about the realm of the resurrected, and not been homesick from that hour, waiting and looking forward joyfully to being released from bodily existence.*
>
> *Whether we are young or old makes no difference. What are twenty or thirty or fifty years in the sight of God? And which of us knows how near he or she may already be to the goal? That life only really begins when it ends here on earth, that all that is here is only the prologue before the curtain goes up-that is for young and old alike to think about. Why are we so afraid when we think about death?... Death is only dreadful for those who live in dread and fear of it. Death is not wild and terrible, if only we can be still and hold fast to God's Word. Death is not bitter, if we have not become bitter ourselves. Death is grace, the greatest gift of grace that God gives to people who believe in him. Death is mild, death is sweet and gentle, it beckons to us with heavenly power, if only we realize that it is the gateway to our homeland, the tabernacle of joy, the everlasting kingdom of peace.*
>
> *How do we know that dying is so dreadful? Who knows whether in our human fear and anguish we are only shivering and shuddering at the most glorious, heavenly, blessed event in the world?*
>
> *Death is hell and night and cold, if it is not transformed by our faith. But that is just what is so marvelous, that we can transform death."[26]*

[21] Eric, Metaxas . *Bonhoeffer: Pastor, Prophet, Martyr, Spy.* Nashville: Thomas Nelson, 2010. P.12
[22] Ibid. P.39
[23] Ibid. P.155
[24] Ibid. P.321
[25] D.J.,Atkinson *New Dictionary of Christian Ethics and Pastoral Theology,* Downers Grove: Intervarsity Press, 1995. P.198
[26] Eric,Metaxas. *Bonhoeffer: Pastor, Prophet, Martyr, Spy.* Nashville: Thomas Nelson, 2010. P.531

There are not two greater (at least in the modern world) idols than that of athletics and academia. While "Chariots of Fire" indeed imports and imposes many modern features into the 1920's, sports in general, "Muscular Christianity" in particular certainly had already loomed large, even as early as 1857.[27] Long lists of "Muscular Christians" inclusive of notables the likes of Billy Sunday, C.T. Studd, Gil Dodds and Eric Liddell have made evangelical and fundamentalist Christianity fertile ground to be hijacked.[28] The fact is, Liddell was indeed quite the athlete, for in addition to his renown as a runner, he also was quite an accomplished rugby player.[29] His recreational pursuits, including his expertise at billiards, was among those he felt (he was good enough at that) he'd "have been happy to make his living playing".[30] Liddell was what we'd call today, "a natural".[31] Yet in all the opportunities to permanently detour and or otherwise derail his life's "purpose" and mission to China, Liddell remained duty bound. As a segue into the world of academia so very familiar to Bonhoeffer, if there was anything Liddell wasn't, it was an intellectual or academician, or even a gifted communicator for that matter.

> *"And an unnamed internee wrote in a personal diary: He was not particularly clever, and conspicuously able, but he was good. He was naturally reserved and tended to live in a world of his own, but he gave of himself unstintedly. His reserve did not prevent him from mixing with everybody and being known by everybody, but he always shrank from revealing his deepest needs and distresses, so that whilst he bore the burdens of many, very few could help to bear his.*
>
> *His fame as an athlete helped him a good deal. He certainly didn't look like a great runner, but the fact that he had been one gave him a self confidence that men of his type don't often have. He wasn't a great leader, or an inspired thinker, but he knew what he ought to do, and he did it. He was a true disciple of the Master and worthy of the highest places amongst the saints gathered in the Church triumphant. We have lost of our best, but we have gained a fragrant memory."[32]*

Eulogized by a roommate, and British businessman, it was said "he lived a far better life than his preaching".[33]

The world of learning, teaching, and preaching was the world of Dietrich Bonhoeffer. His doctoral dissertation was entitled "Sanctorum Communio: A Dogmatic Inquiry into the Sociology of the Church".[34] The mind that produced that dissertation and his vast other academic accomplishment and achievements was "always thinking about thinking".[35] Yet Bonhoeffer never made thinking or theology his idol. He "was not interested in intellectual abstraction", and "theology must lead to the practical aspects of how to live as a

---

[27] Tony,Ladd and James Mathisen. *Muscular Christianity: Evangelical Protestants and the Development of American Sport*. Grand Rapids: Baker Books, 1999. P.14

[28] Ibid. P.214

[29] David, McCasland. *Eric Liddell, Pure Gold*. Grand Rapids: Discovery House, 2001. P.57

[30] Ibid. P.158

[31] Sally, Magnusson. *The Flying Scotsman*. New York: Quartet Books, 1981. P.25

[32] David, McCasland. *Eric Liddell, Pure Gold*. Grand Rapids: Discovery House, 2001. P.285

[33] Ibid. P.285

[34] Eric,Metaxas. *Bonhoeffer: Pastor, Prophet, Martyr, Spy*. Nashville: Thomas Nelson, 2010. P.63

[35] Ibid. P.70

Christian".[36] Bonhoeffer was a major believer in what we today might call "putting truth into shoe leather":

> *"All his life, Bonhoeffer had applied the same logic to theological issues that his father applied to scientific issues. There was only one reality, and Christ was Lord over all of it or none. A major theme for Bonhoeffer was that every Christian must be "fully human" by bringing God into his whole life, not merely into some "spiritual" realm. To be an ethereal figure who merely talked about God, but somehow refused to get his hands dirty in the real world in which God had placed him, was bad theology. Through Christ, God had shown that he meant us to be in this world and to obey him with our actions in this world. So Bonhoeffer would get his hands dirty, not because he had grown impatient, but because God was speaking to him about further steps to obedience."[37]*

As can be seen, while Liddell and Bonhoeffer surely had the means and goods to easily devote themselves, even make an idol of athletics and academics respectively, each mastered the challenge by heeding the call to a higher purpose. The call of, and to, faithful obedience to their supreme master and commander-in-chief, Christ Jesus. They would serve their generation by giving their all to Him and His will in time of great peril.

Discipleship in an Age of Dictators

As has been briefly depicted, Liddell and Bonhoeffer were disciples of Jesus Christ whose commitment to calling in Christ trumped any and every temptation to make a mere idol of either athletics or academia. Theirs was call and commitment to follow Christ. The setting and landscape in which they would be challenged was the land of their birth. For Liddell that was China, for Bonhoeffer, Germany. We in and of the West are far more familiar with the Nazis, Hitler and Germany than we are with the Imperial Emperors of China and Japan. Yet each of those locations and the political affiliations of their day ushered in an anti-christian totalitarianism against which Liddell and Bonhoeffer would emerge as enemy combatants. In each case, they were as wise as serpents, and as innocent as doves, (Matthew 10:16) at least initially. Liddell served for years as a tent maker missionary, "sharing in the religious work, as well as teach(ing) science and supervise(ing) athletics".[38] Though communism was already emerging in China in the 1920's,[39] it wasn't until 1945, (and Japan's defeat) that Mao Zedong really began to hold sway. The final eight years of Liddell's life were concerning with combating the deplorable conditions of rural China with its grinding poverty, coupled with the increasing menacing encroachment[40] and later internment in and at the hand of the Japanese and their encampments (1937-1945).[41] Long before his encampment in 1943, Flo and the children had set sail, (1941) for safety in Canada.[42] Liddell's discipleship meant commitment to the people of China and separation from his wife and family. A third daughter, Maureen, who he would never live to see, was born shortly after their separation.[43] Caught in the cross-fire between would be dictators in Japan and China, Eric Liddell's discipleship enabled him to persevere.

---

[36] Eric, Metaxas . *Bonhoeffer: Pastor, Prophet, Martyr, Spy.* Nashville: Thomas Nelson, 2010. P.129
[37] Ibid. P.361
[38] Sally, Magnusson. *The Flying Scotsman.* New York: Quartet Books, 1981. P.75
[39] Ibid. P.92
[40] Ibid. P.118
[41] Ibid. P.149
[42] Ibid. P.138
[43] Ibid. P.138

Bonhoeffer's extensive dealings, theologically and personally with the threat of Hitler and Nazism are well documented by Metaxas.[44] Evolving as one whose name notably is synonymous with ethics but one widely considered to be a pacifist into a co-conspirator in an assassination attempt represents quite a journey.[45] Like Liddell, Bonhoeffer's commitment to his people in the face of a totalitarian danger and monster was not personally cost free. He would be imprisoned in April 1943[46] and executed on April 9th, 1945, "entirely submissive to the will of God".[47] His engagement to Maria Von Wedemeyer[48] ended (with his death) before the marriage could be consummated.

Surrender and Submission

Answering a higher calling than that of athletics or academia, Liddell and Bonhoeffer were disciples to the end. Each had a marvelous testimony of surrender and submission. Each spent several months enduring the hardship of prison; with all the fear, loneliness, deprivation, and doubt that prisons afford. Long gone were the lights and glamour of the stadium, the track, the classroom, and the pulpit. Given only to visions in memory was the presence of loved ones. In the month before Liddell died he was still living out and teaching submission.

> *"As we start this course of readings we should first surrender our lives to God and dedicate ourselves to doing His will. God's will is only revealed to us step by step. He reveals more as we obey what we know. Surrender means that we are prepared to follow God's guidance, whatever or however He guides, no matter what the cost."* [49]

Liddell passed on February 21, 1945, fully surrendered.

Bonhoeffer 's end came not by something going horribly wrong in his body, but by something going horribly wrong in the world, with his death sentence "almost certainly by decree from Hitler himself".[50] An eye witness provided this riveting account of his execution.

> *" I was most deeply moved by the way this lovable man prayed, so devout and so certain that God heard his prayer. At the place of execution, he again said a short prayer and then climbed the steps to the gallows, brave and composed. His death ensued after a few seconds. In the almost fifty years that I worked as a doctor, I have hardly ever seen a man die so entirely submissive to the will of God."*[51]

Summary and Inspiration

---

[44] Eric,Metaxas. *Bonhoeffer: Pastor, Prophet, Martyr, Spy*. Nashville: Thomas Nelson, 2010. P.425

[45] Ibid. P.358

[46] Ibid. P.441

[47] Ibid. P.532

[48] Ibid. P.433

[49] David, McCasland. *Eric Liddell, Pure Gold*. Grand Rapids: Discovery House, 2001. P.279

[50] Eric,Metaxas. *Bonhoeffer: Pastor, Prophet, Martyr, Spy*. Nashville: Thomas Nelson, 2010. P.529

[51] Ibid. P.532

Two men, precious sons of Zion, showed us the way to live and die for Christ. Theirs was a stage and setting wherein deep and dark forces were at play. Because their lives were given unto Christ, theirs were lives of submission and surrender. As such they were and are real inspiration for us upon whom similar dark clouds gather, and a new dark age will likely emerge. As those clouds and the oppressive anti-Christian totalitarianism continues to gather in the once free West, we too will be faced with prisons, both literal and figurative in which to live out our days. As Rasmussen and others have sought to reveal the significance of the likes of Bonhoeffer for North Americans, he rightly enjoins that we return to a theology of the cross. He wrongly though pits the theology of the cross against the theology of glory.[52] They are clearly two sides of the same coin. I submit that Liddell and Bonhoeffer knew (and know) both. St. Peter, being led where he "would not", certainly links suffering and glory. Finally, our Lord Jesus must be understood in His humiliation as well as in His exaltation. Remember Hebrews 12:2 …"…who for the joy set before him, endured the cross and despised the shame". Liddell and Bonhoeffer offer the same; to see only their sad earthly ending is not to see the whole story and the fuller picture. Though those precious sons, who were comparable to fine gold, were esteemed as mere earthen vessels, they are raised, and their suffering and glory has been and continues to be an inspiration to the countless thousands that have followed, even spanning generations.

Dear LORD, "While we are most thankful for these two, and the countless others that You have sent, please do send us more Precious Sons and Daughters!" And all God's people say, "Amen!"

---

[52] Larry, Rasmussen with Renate Bethage. *Dietrich Bonhoeffer:His Significance for North Americans,* Minneapolis: Fortress Press 1990. P.173

Bibliography/Sources

Atkinson D.J. *New Dictionary of Christian Ethics and Pastoral Theology,* Downers Grove: Intervarsity Press, 1995.

Barnett, Victoria. *Bonhoeffer. A Biography,* Philadelphia: Fortress Press, 2000.

Douglas, J.D., ed. *The New International Dictionary of the* Christian *Church,* Grand Rapids: Zondervan, 1974.

Keddie, John. *Running the Race.* Darlington: Evangelical Press, 2007.

Ladd, Tony and James Mathisen. *Muscular Christianity: Evangelical Protestants and the Development of American Sport.* Grand Rapids: Baker Books, 1999.

Magnusson, Sally. *The Flying Scotsman.* New York: Quartet Books, 1981.

McCasland, David. *Eric Liddell, Pure Gold.* Grand Rapids: Discovery House, 2001.

Metaxas, Eric. *Bonhoeffer: Pastor, Prophet, Martyr, Spy.* Nashville: Thomas Nelson, 2010.

Moreau, Scott A. *Evangelical Dictionary of World Missions.* Grand Rapids: Baker Books, 2000.

Rasmussen, Larry with Renate Bethage. *Dietrich Bonhoeffer:His Significance for North Americans,* Minneapolis: Fortress Press 1990.

Swift, Catherine. *Eric Liddell.* Minneapolis: Bethany House, 1990.

Thompson, David P. *Scotland's Greatest Athlete.* Crieff: The Research Unit, 1970.

Weikhart, Richard. *The Myth of Dietrich Bonhoeffer: Is His Theology Evangelical?* Lanham: International Scholars Publication, 1997.

Wilson, Julian. *Complete Surrender.* United Kingdom: Authentic Media, 2012.

Wright, David F. *The Dictionary of Scottish Church History and Theology.* Edited by Nigel M. De S. Cameron. Downers Grove: Intervarsity, 1993.

Blogs:
Green, Clifford. *Hijacking Bonhoeffer.* The Christian Century, October 5, 2010. The Thoughtful Christian.com
Henebury, Paul Martin. *Dr. Reluctant: "What to think about Dietrich Bonhoeffer"?* WordPress.com

Papers:
Cashmore, Ellis. *Chariots of Fire: Bigotry, Manhood and Moral Certitude in an Age of Individualism.* Sports in Society: Cultures, Commerce, Media, Politics, 11:2-3; 159-173. (2008)

Weikhart, Richard. *"Metaxas's Counterfeit Bonhoeffer: An Evangelical Critique".* California State University, Stanislaus.

www.ingramcontent.com/pod-product-compliance
Lightning Source LLC
Chambersburg PA
CBHW081234020426
42331CB00012B/3166